T0328869

Alexander Scott, Montgomerie, and
Drummond of Hawthornden as
Lyric Poets

Alexander Scott, Montgomerie, and Drummond of Hawthornden as Lyric Poets

Lord Rector's Prize, 1911–12

By
Catharine M. Maclean, M.A.

Advienne que pourra

Cambridge:
at the University Press
1915

CAMBRIDGE
UNIVERSITY PRESS

University Printing House, Cambridge CB2 8BS, United Kingdom

Cambridge University Press is part of the University of Cambridge.

It furthers the University's mission by disseminating knowledge in the pursuit of education, learning and research at the highest international levels of excellence.

www.cambridge.org
Information on this title: www.cambridge.org/9781316509555

© Cambridge University Press 1915

First published 1915
First paperback edition 2015

A catalogue record for this publication is available from the British Library

ISBN 978-1-316-50955-5 Paperback

PREFACE

THE subject of this essay, which gained the Lord Rector's Prize in Edinburgh University in 1912, was selected by the late Mr Wyndham, when Lord Rector of the University in that year.

The author may not publish it without acknowledging the indebtedness of the latter part of the essay to the investigations of Professor Kastner on Drummond, published in 1911 in the *Modern Language Review*.

Acknowledgments are also due to the publishers of the Poems of Rachel Annand Taylor for permission to make quotation from *The Daughter of Herodias*.

CATHARINE M. MACLEAN

December 1914

SCOTT, MONTGOMERIE AND DRUMMOND AS LYRIC POETS

IT is very probable that, as has been suggested in modern times, the impulse when under the stress of emotional excitation to repeat over and over again the same words, has given rise to rhythmical, and, more particularly, to lyrical structure. In connection with this theory it is of significance that all Greek lyrics, most Latin lyrics, and most Elizabethan lyrics were intended to be sung—harmony of notes and harmony of words thus blending into a perfect medium for the interpretation of emotional experience.

Middle Scots as a language was artificial, and in it the lyrical note is somewhat subordinate. There are various anonymous lyrics to be found in the Bannatyne and Maitland MSS, but the chief Middle Scots poets, Henryson, Dunbar, Douglas and Lyndsay, were not primarily lyrical, although in Henryson and Dunbar the pure lyrical note is by no means lacking. The appearance towards the close of Middle Scots of two poets, Montgomerie and Scott, who are lyrical or nothing, is therefore of peculiar interest. That Middle Scots as a language is not characteristically lyrical, is in the first place the result of the distinctive linguistic features of Middle Scots, and in the second, of its literary origin.

The appearance of the beautiful and artificial language called Middle Scots is a curious and an almost unparalleled literary phenomenon. While the blood of all the other dialects in England was being sucked into the London dialect, the Northumbrian dialect north of the Tweed received a new lease of life. The means whereby the palingenesis of the Northern dialect in Scotland was effected, were those of accretion and deliberate selection. Unconsciously the methods which Du Bellay advocated in the *Défense et Illustration de la Langue Française* were adopted. The language was so base and poor, that it had need of ornament, of "les plumes d'autrui," and richly did it help itself to the treasures of other languages. On account of the slenderness of the original stock, the new words were for some time scarcely naturalised, and in consequence a language was produced, varied, it is true, in the different groups of texts, but essentially literary, artificial, stationary and particularly suited for the chryselephantine style of composition. The words had not time to gather round them the charm of tradition and of long association— and thus—although Middle Scots had plenty of variety, force and picturesqueness—it fell into disuse as a literary language shortly after it had become sufficiently mature to be a lyrical instrument.

If from a linguistic point of view Middle Scots was not promising as a lyrical language— still less was it so traditionally. Middle Scots may practically be said to have been called into being by Southern, and particularly by alle- gorical tradition—a tradition which afterwards it restored to the languishing literature of England, the allegory of Douglas leading on pictorially and metrically and spiritually to the allegory of Spenser. Middle Scots incorporated little or nothing of the popular lyric poetry of England—of the plaintive Middle English love poems with their poignant stab—their longing that is almost a pang—but the line of texts which goes to prove the development of Middle Scots from Southern models of a heavier nature is quite clearly defined. The feeble flame of Northern English was prevented from total extinction by the transcription of Southern texts, or by literary compositions in the Southern dialect, probably, if we follow the guiding of inference, by the school of James I. In the transition texts, *Lancelot of the Laik* and the *Quair of Jelousy*, we get Northernisms and pseudo-Southernisms which are necessary for the metre. This justifies the inference that the poems, written in the Southern dialect by one imperfectly acquainted with the Southern dialect, were transcribed by a Northerner. In the *Court of Love* we get both Southernisms and Northernisms. This again points to a Northern scribe. The scribe who has given us *Barbour* has also given us *The Flower and the Leaf* and *The Complaynt of the Black Knight*. In these there are the Northernisms, but not the pseudo-Southernisms. The Northern element is static. The pseudo-Southernisms are lacking when the manuscript is genuinely Southern. This proves the transcription by a Northern scribe of manuscripts both genuinely Southern and pseudo-Southern.

When we come to the *Kingis Quair* the same thing happens. The pseudo-Southernisms are necessary to the metre—the Northernisms are not—and the *Kingis Quair*, transcribed by a Northern scribe, has practically been proved to have been written by James I, that is by one imperfectly acquainted with the Southern dialect.

Thus Northern English was prevented in Scotland from dying out—by transcription of Southern texts; while also the works of a school of anonymous Scottish poets—including the authors of the transition texts, and James the First—writing in a would-be Southern dialect, and therefore full of pseudo-Southernisms, were diligently copied by Northern scribes, who introduced Northernisms detrimental to metre and to euphony.

When James I returned to Scotland the tradition, which had been maturing, fructified on Scottish soil. The vernacular had been gradually changing, and from the grafting on to this changed vernacular of a literary tradition for which a garment of words had to be found, Middle Scots developed rapidly.

The literary origin of Middle Scots then as well as the linguistic idiosyncrasies of the language accounts for the discouragement of the lyrical element, and for the florescence of the allegorical element, the element most emphasised in the transition period. All Middle Scots is mediaeval. Middle Scots does not come into being until the truest mediaeval art—until in fact the conventions of mediaeval art—had been established. It does not share in the Renaissance. Its flame pales in the light of the Renaissance. The last great allegory coloured by the Catholic faith was *King Hart*—and for a time it looked as if the partial dissatisfaction with the allegorical motive would bridge the gulf between Middle Scots and the Renaissance. The minor poetry of Montgomerie bears the marks of contact with the Pléiade. Stuart translated *Orlando Furioso*, and Fowler translated Petrarch and Machiavelli. Yet all these were genuinely mediaeval in spirit; while Drummond—the man who might, if he had had the courage, have turned the rich if somewhat sluggish and turgid stream of Middle Scots into the mainstream of English literature, and thus invested the vocabulary of English poetry with new efficacy and virtue—disowned the literary tradition of his predecessors, left Middle Scots in a petrified condition, a monumental and frozen literature; sold his birthright for the indistinctive heritage of Petrarchian sonnet warbling; with what seems to have been temperamental ineffectiveness, turned his attention so completely to literary composition in the approved Elizabethan style, that he can be called a Middle Scots poet in no sense of the word. He is merely one of the multitudinous contributors to the Elizabethan sweet-toned "gale of song."

And yet there is a difference between Middle Scots at its inception and at its close. The Reformation disturbed somewhat the enthusiasm for allegory—the traditional Catholic conception of life. It called into play the forces of disintegration and disturbed the monotonous conventionalised richness of Middle Scots. Although Middle Scots never partook of the Renaissance, Scott dared to be purely lyrical—to emulate not the architectural and pictorial magnificences of the allegorical school, but the slighter forms of poetry—even to bring into his poetry some of the wild, sweet, half artificial cadences of Middle English lyric, or the courtly stiffness and regularity of the elegant rhymers of Tottel's *Miscellany*; while the lyrical nature of Montgomerie's inspiration even breaks through the conventional allegorical form of *The Cherrie and the Slae*.

It may be well, before proceeding to critical judgment, to make a statement of our general conception of lyric poetry, and of the particular conception of the various kinds of lyric poetry kept in the mind in estimating the poetry of Alexander Scott, Montgomerie and Drummond of Hawthornden.

The best lyric poetry is the expression of powerful feeling. But the presence of strong emotion is not the *differentia* of lyric poetry. Form is the actual *differentia* of the lyric. The lyric poem must be independent of environment, clear cut, complete in itself. The necessity of this may be illustrated from well-known passages in Elizabethan drama.

In the drama or in the epic there may be lyrical passages, but these for reasons of proportion should not be lyrics. If they can legitimately be called lyrics, the drama or epic in which they occur is not properly proportioned; for in what may be called the architectural forms of poetry the parts must be subordinate to the whole—the ornament to the mass—while the essence of the lyric is that it is complete—worthy of consideration on its own merits, perfect in itself—an artistic entity. Short—usually the expression of a particular mood or sentiment, the embodiment of one moment of inspired vision—it occupies for the moment the complete stage.

When Brachiano in *The White Devil* says:

Thou hast led me, like an heathen sacrifice,
With music and with fatal yokes of flowers
To my eternal ruin; woman to man
Is either a god or a wolf,

and shortly afterwards exclaims:

> I have drunk Lethe, Vittoria,
> My dearest happiness, Vittoria,

he is expressing himself in a manner eminently lyrical. But the lines are not segregate. Subordinate as they are to the rest of the passage, they are not developed. Their lyrical possibilities remain in embryo.

The lines of Ford:

> One kiss on those cold lips, my last

or:

> They are the silent griefs that crack the heart-
>   strings;
> Let me die smiling

come, in their fierce emotion, little short of sublimity, but though lyrical, they have not the complete independence of the lyric.

Othello, goaded to frenzy by the malign combination of charm—and (as he supposes) of moral obliquity in Desdemona, exclaims:

> O thou weed,
> Who art so lovely fair and smell'st so sweet
> That the sense aches at thee, would thou hadst
>   ne'er been born!

These lines, lyrical in sentiment and expression, and inclined to draw attention to themselves to the detriment of dramatic proportion, have been censured from a dramatic standpoint—and yet undeveloped as they are they cannot be said to constitute lyric. Lyrical expression is given to the idea embodied in them, the sense of the combination of beauty and impurity—when Rachel Annand Taylor isolates and elaborates the sentiment, and writes:

> The daughter of Herodias,
> She danced before the King:
> That rain of ecstasy she was
> Whose silver and fantastic feet
> Flash down the ways of Spring.

> The daughter of Herodias,
> She danced in gold and red
> Upon the floor of chrysopras:—
> The light of flaming cities broke
> Behind her sumptuous head.

> The daughter of Herodias
> Resplendent, unappalled,
> Wove such a spell, it came to pass
> She drew the soul down sounding seas
> Of pearl and emerald.

> O daughter of Herodias
> What horror of the deep,
> What shine of impure things !—alas !
> What loathing, loathed captivities
> In that abysmal sleep!

Not only is lyric independent, and clear-cut in form. Lyric poetry very largely is form, sheer form. Form in lyric and idea in lyric are partly synonymous. In the finest lyrics, form and thought are indivisible—for in the wild endeavour to seize within the web of art the subtlest thought and the most gossamer emotion, the form becomes, to adopt a metaphor from ancient Egyptian sepulchral belief, but a luminousness surrounding and interpenetrating the soul of the lyric. The ideal lyric is isolated—beautiful in form—beautiful in its entirety—having words, ornament, rhythm and all decorative accessories contributing to, and subordinate to, the general effect.

In both ancient and modern literature lyrics have been of two kinds—lyrics of passion, in which the poet, after what Gautier calls "la lutte acharnée," has pent within the prison-house of words his emotional apprehension of things, lyrics which, to quote Bacon, are "drenched in flesh and blood," which retain something of the breathlessness of the struggle for expression—and lyrics courtly, polished and beautiful, expressions of light feeling, attaining their rank by their clearness, their brilliant flawlessness, their hard perfection of artistic "composition," lyrics like those of Anacreon which fascinated the Pléiade. But in all the best lyrics passion is seldom wanting. The qualitative range of the passion is very wide.

There may be the passion of tortured emotion crying out for self-externalisation—or the passion of a pagan and joyous apprehension of the daring colours on life's canvas, or the peculiar languid passion of the quietist, or (and in dealing with the more formal kinds of lyric of Elizabethan England or the scanty lyric of Middle Scots this must certainly be kept in mind) the sheer passion for words, for linguistic reverie—for essays in verbal psychology, or in metrical experiment, which has led to the production of some of the richest and most sumptuous of our lyrics.

The motives most fertile of lyrical accomplishment are those of love and war—of the sense of the beauty of things—of the sense of the pity of things—and of delight in nature. Most of the lyrics of the Renaissance and of mediaeval times may be referred to one or another of these.

It is difficult to understand the very high praise that is sometimes given to the poems of Alexander Scott. At his best, Scott has a good deal of lyrical charm, but for sustained poetic virtue he is not to be compared to Montgomerie. Metrically he was a disciple of Dunbar—and pale indeed does the literary personality of the disciple look beside the rich and distinctive personality of the Master.

The best lyrical elements of the poetry that preceded his own, Scott failed to incorporate in his work. In him there is nothing like the winsome lightness of *Robene and Makeyne*—or of the beauty of *The Bludy Sark*. He does not elaborate the motives so fruitful in the cases of Dunbar and Villon—of the ephemerality of all things, of the fear of the unknown, a motive that had been elaborated in many a wild and plaintive cadence. But enough of disparagement!

Any genius that Scott had was lyrical. Scott was lyrical or nothing. In an age of allegorical convention and of mediaeval chivalry he broke through the allegorical tradition on the one hand, and the traditions of chivalry on the other.

The specific lyrical quality of Scott, whatever it be, is not that of emotional richness or intensity. The pleasure derived is rarely that of emotional excitation.

In the creation of formal beauty, however, independent of the alchemy of passion, Scott excels. In metrical invention he was fertile. In thirty-six poems he employs twenty-six kinds of metre. The characteristics of the old school of metrists are curiously mingled with the graceful amatory trifling of the school of Surrey.

A competent metrist, Scott understood the management of what may be called the accessories of form—and knew how to weave quaint phrases and fine rhythm into an aesthetically satisfying whole. The feeling for words indispensable to a lyrist was his in no small degree. The rich vocabulary of Middle Scots lost nothing at his hands. His poems are full of quaint felicities of diction. So far as was possible, he applied the poetical stores of Middle Scots to lyrical use. He employs stock words which had come through the mill of the older poets and had originally been borrowed from Chaucer—words like "on rys" and "dowsy peres," and when writing in the "full-dress" style employs many a resonant Latinism. Scott's instinct for good and vivid words was keener than that of Montgomerie, who does not disdain to borrow from him. Some of the best of his words are: "belappit," "blay-knit," "fyrefangit," "reidwod," "womenting" (afterwards employed by Spenser), "bruckill" (likewise adopted by Spenser), "monebrunt," and "wappit" as in the lines:

> Wappit without recure
> In wo remidiles.

The quality of his ornate phrasing may be judged from the following examples:

> With pensyve hairt opprest.
> Blandit with eloquence.
> Fair prefulgent visage bricht,

while the lines:

> And hornit Dyane with her paly glemis
> Perssis the cluddis sabill in the nicht,

might have come from one of the prologues to the *Aeneid*.

Scott is always happy in his use of alliteration and of alliterative cadences. His tastefulness in this respect may be illustrated from the following lines:

> Ane rubent roiss upon þe ryce.
> To mak braid Britane blyth as bird on breir.
> Some monebrunt madynis myld.
> In gardyns grene their grass to glaid.
> Her glistring garments are so gay.
> Bene vaneist with the wind.
> Under that redolent roiss tree.
> Passis the wallowit weidis in the vail.
> Quhair mirthles I wes marterit oft.

The themes which inspired Scott's verse were: war, politics, the popular love tale (either as a motive of satire or of conventional melancholy), and religion.

Of the last, little need be said—Scott's two attempts at translation of the Psalms were entirely negative in quality.

The New Yeir Gift to Quene Mary—the one political composition—is different from the other poems. It is heavily aureated. It is, in fact, of chryselephantine workmanship—full of Latinisms and alliteration. The envoy illustrates the *engouement* for internal rhymes:

> Prudent, maist gent, tak tent and prent þe wordis,
> Intill this bill with will thame still to face
> Quhilkis are not skar to bar on far fra bawrdis,
> Bot leale, but feale, may haell avaell thy Grace,

which, when exhibited by Marot, who probably influenced Scott, in such a passage as:

> La blanche colombelle belle
> Souvent je noys priant criant,
> Mais dessoulz la cordelle d'elle
> Me jett un œil friant riant,

aroused the contempt of Ronsard.

The alliteration is richest in the closing lines of the poem:

> Fresch fulgent flurist fragrant flour formois,
> Lantern to luf, of ladeis lamp and lot,
> Cherie maist chaist, cheif charbucle and chois,
> Smaill sweit smaragde, smelling but smit of smot.

The popular motive is exemplified in the *Justing and Debait*; Scotland was rich in that kind of tale. Even before the influence of Chaucer had penetrated to Scotland, the humorous tale had a distinctive place in the heart of the people.

This kind of tale does not bear on lyrical production except metrically. The metre almost always has a certain force and swing, exemplified in these lines from *The Ballat of Matrimony*:

> And if thou wilt not work, quod he,
> Thou drab, I shall thee drive.
> I would to God, thou knave, quod she,
> Thou durst that matter pryve.

From *Christis Kirk*, the classical specimen of this method of depicting the humours of low life, through the poetry of Dunbar and Lyndsay, there is a continual succession of tales of this kind, leading on to the *Justing and Debait*. Mr Chesterton has said that "all over the world, the folk literature, the popular literature is the same," that "it consists of very dignified sorrow and of very undignified fun," its sad tales being of "broken hearts, its happy tales of broken heads." The melancholy side of popular literature is usually a fertile lyrical motive, but the comic side is inimical to the lyrical spirit. The humour, the realism and the spirited manner of the *Justing and Debait* are splendid, but the light, competent metre, the eight-lined octosyllabic stanza with bob and wheel, is the only lyrically significant feature of it.

As might be expected, the amatory motive is the most fertile of the four. In his writings on love and women, Scott has two moods. In one of them he gives rein to that streak of violence and intellectual horse-play not uncommon in Scottish literature. In this mood he is personal, not an adherent of any school, full of pungency and of cynicism that stings like a blow. When writing in this vein he can hardly be called lyrical, for the play of the critical spirit and the flaming of the ironical passion are not conducive to lyrical excellence. Scott is bitter rather than passionate. If he were passionate his passion would have invested even his abuse with the lyrical throb—as Polwart's did his in the last Flyting. The extraordinary stock of words brutal and idiosyncratic at his command is as cold as it is coarse, and licence of vocabulary kills the instinct for beauty.

Poems like *The Slicht Remeid of Love* and *Ane Ballat made to the Derisioun and Scorne of Wantoun Women* belong to no school of poetry. They anticipate the violence and insolent idiosyncrasy of Donne. *Of Wemenkynd; In June the Jem; Returne thee, Hairt* and *Ye blindit Luvaris, luk,* are written in a spirit of revolt against the tradition of deference imposed on the courtly

lover. These words in *In June the Jem* give the
substance of the revolt:

> I maik it plane
> For love agane
> Their sall no sorrow in me synk;
> Nor ʒit in vane
> To suffer pane
> To stop from sleip, frome meit or drink.
> Thair is no lady fre
> That, and scho favour me,
> Scho will nocht thoill to se
> Me pyne, I think,

and again we have the lines:

> Quhen scho growis heich
> I draw on dreich
> To vesy and behald the end:
> Quhen scho growis skeich
> I byd on beich
> To lat hir in the brydill bend;
> Quhen scho growis meik and tame
> Scho salbe wylcom hame,
> Gif scho my luve quyt clame
> I sall not kend.

But Scott has also a conventional mood, and
in it he is wholly delightful. The poems,
pleasing metrically, are sprinkled with flowers of
vocabulary. The poem on May is very beautiful
as regards both language and metre. The
metrical lilt of *Luve preysis but Comparesone* is
delightful. The three poems on *Hairtis* are good,
even if one of them is a *pastiche*—a piece of

elaborate trifling—and if the conceit is a little far-fetched. The metre of *Quha is perfyte* recalls the soft energy and the lightness of fourteenth century lyrics and carols, especially in the lines:

> That bird of bliss
> In bewty is
> In end the only A per se,
> Quhais mowth to kiss
> Is worth, I wiss,
> The world full of gold to me.
> Is nocht in erd I cure
> Bot pleiss my lady pure
> Syne be hir scheruiture
> Until I de.

The double refrain of *It cumis ʒow Luvaris to be laill*, even if mechanical, is pleasing. It is better still in the lighter poem which follows, as may be seen by the lines:

> Be land or se
> Quhair evir I be
> As ʒe fynd me
> So tak me,
> And gif I le
> And from ʒow fle
> Ay quhill I de
> Forsaik me.

The last verse with its double rhymes is like a crescendo:

> My deir adew
> Most cleir of hew,
> Now on me new
> And so tak me;

Gif I persew
And beis nocht trew
Cheiss ȝe ane new
And forsaik me.

*Only to ȝow in Erd that I lufe best, Rycht as
the Glass bene thirlit thrucht with bemes* and *Up
Helsum Hairt* are stately in metre and elaborate in
diction—belonging to the characteristic metrical
type of Middle Scots. The stanzas in which they
are written are apt to call for a richer vocabulary
than the lyrics of shorter lines.

The mood of conventional melancholy finds
expression in the following poems: *A Luvariss
Complaint; Adew, Luvaris, Adew; Lament of the
Maister of Erskyn; On paciens in Luve; Oppressit
Hairt, Indure; Leif, Luve, and lat me leif allone;
Thocht I in grit Distress; Langour to leive, allace;
Favour is fair; To luve unluvit; Quha lykis to luve;
A Rondel of Luve* and *A Complaint aganis Cupeid.*
The best of these are *Oppressit Hairt, Indure;
A Rondel of Luve* and *To luve unluvit.* There is
genuine passion in the last of these. In it Scott
has apprehended the psychological as distin-
guished from the mechanical use of the refrain.
He had caught something of the inspiration of
Sidney in dealing with the repeated lines. The
refrain acquires fresh force each time it is

repeated. The cumulative effect may be judged from the first two verses:

> To luve unluvit it is ane pane,
> For scho that is my soverane
> Sum wantoun man so he has set hir
> That I can get no lufe agane
> But breke my hairt and nocht the better.
>
> Quhen that I went with that sweit may
> To dance, to sing, to sport and play,
> And oft tymes in my armis plet hir,
> I do now murne both nycht and day
> And breke my hairt and nocht the better.

The refrain is like a dull sob. In this poem the art of Scott is seen at its best—clear cut, lyrical, intellectualised as regards mechanism, having beauty of cadence, of word, and of refrain wrought by what has all the effect of passion into a perfect lyric.

Montgomerie owes a great deal to Scott— yet he was a greater poet. He rose to excellence as great as that of Scott, and his poetic quality is more sustained. Like Scott, he neither vibrates with the pagan delight of the Renaissance, nor with the exuberance of "that amazingly healthy period, when even the lost spirits were hilarious," but in most of his poetry there is genuine emotion. His poems belong to the literature of melancholy. Unlike Scott, he was swayed with "the lyric emotions of the soul," and his poems gain greatly by the impression they give of being the fruit of genuine emotion.

Montgomerie was a very careful metrist. A more prolific poet than Scott, his metres are more varied. He exhibits his competence alike in light intricate lyrical metre, in the heavier stanzas, and in the decasyllabic couplet. In the accessories of metre, too, he is no mean craftsman. His feeling for words is not so keen as that of Scott, from whose distinctive vocabulary he sometimes borrows, but his vocabulary is always tasteful and appropriate. In his sonnets there is something of the love for compound adjectives with which English poetry was infected by French. In one sonnet occur the words "wondrous-vautit," "restless-rolling," and "firme-fixit." Of the technical peculiarities of Middle Scots he takes every advantage. Alliteration he uses with good effect. Perhaps the most distinctive merit of his poetry is the manner in which he managed to invest many of his lines with that peculiar minor melody which runs hauntingly through many a beautiful line of earlier Middle Scots. This beauty of cadence may be illustrated from the following individual lines :

> The mair I wrestlit with the wynd.
> I stakkerit at the windilstrayis.
> With sleikit sophismis seiming smeil.
> Will flatterit him when first he flew.
> Be the mirkness of the moon.

The motives of Montgomerie's verse are the following: allegory, delight in nature, love and religion.

The allegorical motive inspired *The Cherrie and the Slae*—Montgomerie's longest poem. The metre of *The Cherrie and the Slae* is more suitable for lyric than for narrative poetry. Indeed, the poem is lyrical all through. The flexibility of the metre allowing readily the insertion of saw and of argument is worthy of high commendation.

Feeling for nature has inspired some beautiful passages in *The Cherrie and the Slae*, as well as three entire poems: *The Solsequium, The Address to the Sun* and *The Night is neir gone.*

The beauty of the descriptive passages in *The Cherrie and the Slae* is elsewhere unsurpassed in Montgomerie. The most exquisite of these is perhaps the one beginning with the lines:

> The dew in diamondis did hing
> Upon the tender twistis and ȝing
> Ouir-twinkling all the trees,

but the following verse, descriptive of the

cherries which inspired so much argument, is almost as good:

> The Cherries hang abune my heid
> Like twinkland rubies round and reid,
> So hich up in the hewch;
> Quhais schaddowis in the riuer schew
> Als graithlie glansing as they grew
> On twinkling twistis tewch
> Quhilk bowed throw burding of their birth
> Inclining down thair toppis.
> Reflex of Phoebus of the Firth
> Newe colourit all thair knoppis
> With dansing, and glansing,
> In tirles dornik champ,
> Ay streimand and gleimand
> Throu brichtness of that lamp.

The *Solsequium*, recalling a sonnet in its manner, is a very beautiful poem. Most of its charm it acquires from its metre:

> Lyk as the dum
> Solsequium
> With cair ouercum,
> And sorou, when the sun goes out of sight,
> Hings doun his head
> And droops as dead,
> And will not spread
> Bot louks his leavis throu langour of the nicht.

The *Address to the Sun* is a graceful little lyric in *rime couée*. *The Night is neir gone*—written in the lightest of measures—delights by its swing, its freshness and its exuberance. It conveys to the reader the anticipatory thrill aroused by the hour in which everything that lives out of doors seems to stir. The opening of the poem is exuberant:

> Hay, now the day dauis,
> The jolie cok crauis,
> Men shroudis the shauis
> Throu Natur anone;
> The thissel-cok cryis
> On louers vha lyis,
> Nou skaithis the skyis,
> The nicht is neir gone.

All Montgomerie's love poems are contained in the sonnets and in the miscellaneous poems. The love poetry of Montgomerie displays Pléiade influence.

The sonnets are not all amatory. Montgomerie was one of the first poets of the sixteenth century to adopt continental lyrical and sonneteering forms. The sonnets are by no means of uniform quality. The love sonnets were strongly influenced by Ronsard.

The first three sonnets, rather heavy in style, and more aureated than the others, are inspired by religious feeling. In the second sonnet to Mr David Drummond there are some good lines:

> My garland grene is withrit with the wind.
> The cuccou flees before the turtle dove.

The sonnet addressed to the king contains two extremely good lines:

> Thir bluidy sarks cryis alwayis in ʒour eiris,

and

> Upon his heid Caesarean to sett.

There is little distinctive in the sonnets to the *King's Uranie*, except the line:

> Diana with hir boroude beimes and blind.

Not until we come to the sonnets on women and on love do we again get Montgomerie's distinctive and sustained lyrical charm, appearing in such lines as:

> For swetest smell and shyning to the sight.
> Whom should I warie by my wicked weard.
> In hir unhappy hands sho held my heed.
> Bot sigh, and sobbe, and soun, when sho suld
>   sleep.
> Bot once imbarkit, I must byde the blast.

The metre of the last of the group entitled *A Lady's Lamentation* is indeed expressive of the passion of remorse:

> I wyt myn ee for vieuing of my wo,
> I wyt myn earis for heiring my mishap,
> I wyt my senses whilk dissaivit me so,
> I wyt acquentance that in credit crap,
> I wyt the trane that took me with a trap.

The beginning of the first sonnet to Margaret Drummond is very fine; and the first of the sonnets entitled *To The Ferme* is particularly charming, full as it is of harmonious cadences.

The five sonnets *On His Maistress*, which follow, have much more lyrical charm than the average Elizabethan sonnet, particularly the last of them:

> How long sall I in languishing lament?
> How long sall I bot duyne, and do not die?

The love lyrics scattered among the miscellaneous poems may be divided into three main classes: complaints, poems to the poet's mistress, and poems of mild invective against love. The complaints are the most numerous. Their general excellence is high. *A Regrate of Hard Luck in Love* is one of the poorest. Notwithstanding the presence of some very good lines it lacks colour. One of the best is the one entitled *Melancholie, Grit Deput of Despair*. The expansion towards the end into lines internally rhymed is especially good and expressive.

The lyrics to the poet's mistress are all charming. In the lyric called *The Poet reasons with his Mistress* the verse beginning with the lines:

Tak tym in tyme, while tyme is to be tane,
Or ȝe may wish and want it when ȝe wald.
ȝe get no grippe again, if it be gane,
Then, whill ȝe haif it, best is for to hald—

echoes that cry of the French Renaissance:

Cueillez dès aujourd'hui les roses de la vie.

The Poet's Dreme contains the very good line:

The sheirand shaft soon slippit to my hairt.

The poem *In Praise of his Maistress* contains
some very pleasing lines, such as:

Hir browis are brent, lyke golden threeds
Hir silver shyning brees,
The bony blinks my courage feeds
Of hir twa christall ees,
Twinkling illuminous
With beamis amorous,

but its slightly mechanical enumeration of
physical details contrasts unfavourably with the
physical rapture of the poets of the French
Renaissance.

The two poems called *A Deception of Vane
Lovers* and *Against Love* are the fruit of the mood
of revolt against courtly love.

As well as the poems on love there are some
complaints against fortune; two charming poems
on *The Well of Love*, and the pleasing poem,
vaguely reminiscent of Marot, called *Echo*.

The devotional mood in Montgomerie was more productive than in Drummond. There are, of course, the translations of the Psalms— a form of lyrical composition popularised by Marot. These have nothing particularly to commend them. Of the other devotional poems, the one beginning with the lines:

> Away vane world, bewitcher of my hairt
> My soroies shauis, my sins maks me to smairt,

and ending with the lines:

> Let the world be gone, I cair not
> Chryst is my love alone, I feir not—

is the most interesting. It shows how essentially mediaeval Montgomerie was—how superficial in him was the influence of the Renaissance.

Montgomerie's Flytings can hardly be called lyrical compositions, but the provocative repetition in the first Flyting—the ring and lilt in them all—and the excellent treatment of language, entitle them to a certain amount of consideration in estimating his lyrical genius. Very delightful is the lilt of the metre in the *Answer to Polwert*, beginning with the lines:

> Vyle venemous viper, wanthriftest of things,
> Half an elfe, halfe an aipe, of nature deny it.

Some of the passages in the *Answer* become

actually lyrical by the saving grace of rhythm and vocabulary.

Montgomerie is the sweetest of the lyrical poets of Middle Scots. The sweetness of his poetry recalls that of *Robene and Makeyne.* It has been said that he was the first to illustrate the possibilities of Scottish poetry in smoothness, elegance and finish. His poems—full of poignancy—of pale sweetness and of linguistic witchery—retain something of the "divine liquidity" of Chaucer.

In Montgomerie there is both conscious and semi-conscious imitation of foreign models. His mastery over the sonnet—his ability to weave simile, conceit, line and a fourteen-lined rhyme scheme into an artistic entity—points to much study of Italian models.

In Montgomerie's best lyrics there is the caressing note which charms in the lyric of the Pléiade. This is a new note in Scottish poetry.

Montgomerie did not found a lyrical school. Although he drew into his verse all the best lyrical cadences and the lyrical beauties of diction of Middle Scots, the younger poets preferred to turn to the Elizabethans for inspiration. He was the Last of the Makars. "The moth was in the raiment" of Middle Scots poetry.

The beauty of the poetry of Montgomerie may be likened to the beauty of a frayed garment—to the "delicate splendour" that comes before eclipse. It is the swan song of a dying tradition. The florescence of the lyrical impulse in the art of Scott and of Montgomerie was but the glow before the sun of Middle Scots set for ever.

In the case of Drummond we shall postpone any general consideration, except the consideration of the lyrical inspiration and of the form, until the all-important question of plagiarism has been discussed.

Drummond's inspiration was not emotional. For his sonnets indeed there would seem to be a personal reason; but if the death of Mary Cunningham aroused in Drummond personal sorrow and passion he failed to get the burden of his personal message into his verse. He probably had not the strength, in defiance of the tradition of the school he adhered to, to weave his loss and grief into a distinctive symphony—or he had not the heart for the struggle with language which the delivery of a new message always necessitates. His verse just misses being great poetry. He wove for himself a beautiful, rich, and coloured vocabulary, but this vocabulary was garnered from others—not woven out of the struggle of the soul for expression. The beautiful phrases, the elegant harmonies, the "fopperies of diction" not having behind them the driving force of personal conviction, became merely the garment in which Drummond clothed the vague thought and impulses, which in common with his century he possessed.

The form of Drummond's verse is almost unimpeachable. Drummond is lyrical as regards metre, as regards poetical style and as regards vocabulary. Any examination of his sonnets and of those poems of irregular length of line which he calls madrigals, as well as of the longer decasyllabic poems, convinces of his metrical sorcery. The madrigals are particularly charming, although in some of them the rhymes are too far apart—the recollection of the sound of a word having worn off before the word that rhymes with it appears. The chief forms employed are sonnets, sextains, madrigals, songs in couplets sometimes decasyllabic—in couplets sometimes the component lines of which are not of the same length—and hymns of varying form.

Drummond was a stylist. He knew how to compose lines so as to get the utmost value out of each word. This stylistic quality is felt in the single lines which follow:

Triumphant arches, statues crowned with bays.
Look how the flower which lingeringly doth fade.
To shun this rock Capharean of untruth.
Fanes vainly builded to vain idols' praise.
Weep nature, weep: astonish'd world, lament,
  Lament ye winds.
With diamantine sceptre in thy hand.
Hesperian fruit, the spur in you does raise
    That Delian wit that otherwise may sleep.
The Hyperborean bulls, Ceraunus' snow
  Or Arimaspus (cruel!) first thee bred,
    The Caspian tigers with their milk thee fed.

The weakest point in Drummond's formal equipment is his inaccuracy in rhyming. The lyric poet can rarely afford weakness in rhyme. Not being able to rely on the mass, the grandeur, the architectural impressiveness of his work, he should have as his ideal perfection of detail. Poor rhymes occur again and again throughout the body of Drummond's verse. We find such rhymes as east and west, Rome and tomb, thoughts and draughts, bequeath and breath, refuse her and rejoice her, chamber and amber, faces and masses, amphitheatre and water, water and scatter, painted and presented. Inaccuracy of rhyme is the only serious flaw in Drummond's formal excellence.

The accessories of form in Drummond are entirely satisfactory. Drummond has a very full poetic vocabulary. Supremely interested in words, he adopted every means of extending his vocabulary, such as the introduction of French words and the formation of adjectives in imitation of French ones; and as he had the instinct for words without the courage for the strenuous struggle needed for the production of a highly coloured vocabulary, he adopted the methods of plagiarism with regard to vocabulary as well as with regard to idea.

The tendency to borrow contemporary French words is seen in the employment of the following words: phare, umbrage, ramage, collin; and in the tendency to the formation of words by means of prefixes, as in the words embower, ensaffron, disgarland.

Drummond's love for compound adjectives— a love just beginning to awaken in Montgomerie— results in the formation of such adjectives as shrill-sounding, eye-speaking, sweet-sour, heaven-banished, and soul-stinging.

But Drummond added mostly to his vocabulary through the methods of plagiarism, or at least through borrowing. That Drummond was a worshipper of the phrase may be seen from the appearance in *Cypress Grove* of phrases like "raised in the wind of ambition," and "this glorious pageant of the world"; and of sentences like: "How can death be evil, sith it is the thaw of all these vanities which the frost of life bindeth together," or "Life is a journey on a dusty way,—the furthest rest is death."

Devoted as he was to beauty of phrase it is not surprising that he should turn to Sidney, whose sonnets are remarkable for that beauty of phrase which makes us recognise the Sidney of the sonnets as the Sidney of the *Arcadia* and of the *Apology*—and which is the sole justification for the conception of the theory that Sidney, Shakespeare and Bacon are one. Nothing could be more natural than that Drummond should take his unoriginality to drink at the well of Sidney's inspiration—than that the artist, full of critical apprehension of the beauty of phrase, but lacking the power to create, should pilfer from the creative master. As usual, the borrowing is done with artistic unobtrusiveness. Sidney's phrases are woven into the very web of the verse, and no one unacquainted with Sidney's verse would know that they were transplantations. Some of the plagiarisms are:

> But, God wot, wist not what was in my brain.
> Best companied when most I am alone.
> Indifferent host to shepherds and to kings.
> I long to kiss the image of my death.
> These tears, and the black map of all my woe.

O tongue in which most luscious nectar lies.
There flow'rs are spread which names of princes bear.
In colour black to wrap these comets bright.

To give further examples would be pointless, for indeed the entire sequence of Drummond's sonnets is decked out with the flowers of the earlier master's verse. Not only words but ideas and manner are sometimes borrowed.

Nor did Drummond disdain the other sonneteers. From Daniel he derives his fondness for referring to "amber locks," and the exquisite phrase "the April of my years."

Before further discussion of Drummond's poetry is possible, we must now deal with the question of plagiarism in general—a question, any real study of which, would require a very close acquaintance with the French and Italian literature of three centuries. It is difficult to see—in his love poetry at any rate—how Drummond could have failed to plagiarise. Plagiarism had almost become a convention with the school he chose to follow. "I gather my honey as the bees do, from every flower of Parnassus," Ronsard had said; and what in the case of Ronsard was legitimate enrichment became in Elizabethan England unabashed plagiarism. Drummond disowned the old Scottish tradition—the quaint words which by Montgomerie's time had matured and had acquired lyrical charm. He turned away from the fountain of Scottish poetry and had to find a new fountain.

When we have only similarity of idea as a criterion, it is difficult to say exactly what is plagiarism and what is not, for the sonneteering school not only was one complex organism, but the various component parts of the organism were inextricably conjoined, and acted and reacted on each other incessantly. The sonnet spread from Italy to France, yet the later Italians translated the poets of the Pléiade,— and the Elizabethans imitated alike the early and the late Italian poets, and the masters of the Pléiade and their followers.

Drummond had creative tendencies but no power of execution. Instead of forging out for himself, as did the great poets of the Pléiade, a naturalised, individualised and intellectual vocabulary, he merely selected his vocabulary by an artificial process. His intention was probably quite honest—for he borrowed from well-known as well as from obscure models. Recently his plagiarism has been ruthlessly exposed, and perhaps now the tendency is to be too censorious —to convict him of spiritual plagiarism on evidence which, when the diffusion of the sonneteering spirit is considered and the amount of material that was common stock, fails to convict.

Verbal plagiarism is, however, immediately recognisable. Some idea of the parasitic nature of Drummond's genius may be gained by looking through Ward's edition of the poems, and regarding not the borrowings in spirit, but the many borrowings evidently direct from the French and Italian schools. Desportes, himself an inveterate plagiarist, was Drummond's favourite French model. Drummond did not, however, as Lodge did, deliberately rifle the pages of Desportes. He rather reproduces work which has become part of the furniture of his mind. Owing to his passion for words, his sonnets, in their harmony of parts and sumptuous imagery, are invariably better than their original.

The Italian models from whom Drummond borrowed were Tasso, Marino, Luigi-Groto, Serafini and Paterno.

In the sonnet which follows the *Tears on the Death of Moeliades*, the last line,

In whom save death naught mortal was at all,

is taken from a line in one of Guarini's madrigals,

Ne di mortal havesti altro, che morte.

The opening lines of the epitaph sonnet are from Tasso. The remainder of the sonnet comes from Passerat.

The borrowings in the first part of the "poems" are numerous. The sixth sonnet is an adaptation of one of Luigi Groto. The seventh sonnet—Platonic in spirit—is reminiscent both of Sidney and Desportes, in the lines:

> My mind me told that in ane other place
> It elsewhere saw the idea of that face,
> And lov'd a love of heavenly pure delight.

The exquisite sonnet eight was partly from Petrarch. Sonnet nine has been suggested by Marino. The opening lines of sonnet ten are certainly from those of Paterno:

> Luna, che col tuo puro, et freddo argento,
> Sueli a la maggior ombra il fosco horrore,

while the rest of the poem comes from Passerat. The eleventh sonnet is constructed on the pattern of a sonnet of Passerat; the first madrigal was translated from the madrigal by Marino beginning with the lines:

> Fabro dela mia morte
> Sembr io verme ingegnoso
> Che intento al proprio mal mai non riposo.

A model for the thirteenth sonnet is supplied by the thirty-third sonnet of *Diane*, Book I:

Si tost qu'au plus matin ma Diane s'éveille
(O Dieux jugez mon heur,) je suis à son lever
Et voy tout le plus beau qui se puisse trouver
Depuis les Indiens jusqu'où Phoebus sommeille.

The second madrigal is a translation from
Tasso. Part of the nineteenth sonnet is directly
imitated from those lines of Marino:

Ei novo Zeusi, al' Oriente tolto
L' oro, l' ostro al' Aurora, i raggi al Sole
Il bel crin ne figura, e gli occhi e 'l volto.

Sonnet twenty is translated from Desportes,
Œuvres Chrestiennes, XVII:

Quand miroir de moy-meme, en moy je me regarde,
Je noy comme le tans m'est sans fruict escoulé,
Tandis que de jeunesse et d'amour affolé,
Ce monde en ses destours m'amuse et me retarde.

Drummond has improved on his original,
but has strangely enough missed the beautiful
phrase "comme une songe fuyante." Sonnet
thirty-two is practically translated from one of
the sonnets of the *Œuvres Chrestiennes*. Sonnet
thirty-six is practically translated from the
twelfth sonnet of *Les Amours d'Hippolyte*, beginning with the lines:

Celuy qui n'a point veu le printans gracieux
Quand il estale au ciel sa richesse prisée
Remplissant l'air d'odeurs, les herbes de rosée,
Les cœurs d'affections et de larmes les yeux.

.   .   .   .

Qu'il s'arrete pour voir la celeste lumiere
Des yeux de ma deesse, une Venus premiere.

Sonnet thirty-seven was suggested by a composition on the same theme in the sixty-second sonnet of the *Amours* of Ronsard, which begins thus:

Que dis-tu, que fais tu, pensif tourtourelle?

Sonnet forty-six transforms rather a colourless sonnet of Ronsard into a very pleasing one. Sonnet forty-eight reproduces one of the *Amours Diverses*. Drummond translates "doux cheveux," "doux liens," and "doux filets" as "hair, precious hair," "sweet nets," and "dear amulet" respectively. There is no mere mechanical reproduction in Drummond.

The second series of poems owe no less than the first to foreign models. The first and second sonnets are indebted to Marino, the first being obviously a translation of that sonnet of Marino beginning thus:

O d' humano splendor breve baleno.

The fourth sonnet is translated from Sanazzaro.

The beautiful first madrigal, opening so finely with the lines:

> This life which seems so fair
> Is like a bubble blown up in the air
> By sporting children's breath
> Who chase it everywhere,

is altered from the madrigal of Guarini, no whit less fine, entitled *Humana fragilita*. That sonnet of Desportes which begins with the lines:

> Voici du gay printans l'heureux advenement,
> Qui fait que l'hyver morne à regret se retire,
> Déjà la petite herbe, au gré du doux zéphire
> Navré de son amour branle tout doucement,

is the model of the ninth sonnet of Drummond; and that of the *Diane*, which opens thus:

> Las que me sert de voir ces belles plaines
> Pleines de fruits, d'arbrisseaux et de fleurs,
> De voir ces prez bigarrez de couleurs
> Et l'argent vif des bruyantes fontaines,

suggested Drummond's tenth sonnet.

Madrigal three is translated from the madrigal of Guarini entitled *Bella Donna Campala*; madrigal four and the twelfth sonnet from Tasso.

Song two, one of the finest as well as the most philosophical of Drummond's pieces—opposed in spirit to the poetry which sings of the things of this life—is largely an adaptation of a portion of the *Phaedo*.

Not less distinguished by their tendency to help themselves to the fruits of the exertions of others, linguistic and philosophical, are the *Spiritual Poems*. The beautiful sonnet beginning with the lines

Come forth, come forth, ye blest triumphing bands,

and the sonnet beginning with the lines:

Thrice happy he who by some shady grove
Far from the clamorous world doth live his own,

are adapted from Marino.

Plagiarism in the division of poems entitled "Madrigals and Epigrams" is greatly to be excused, as much of the material for epigrams was classical common stock. *The Statue of Medusa* is suggested by an epigram of Tebaldeo; *Of Phyllis* is borrowed from a madrigal of Guarini; *The Cannon* comes from Serafini; the epigram beginning with the lines:

World, wonder not that I
Engrave thus in my heart
This angel face which me bereaves of rest,

was suggested by Passerat. *Of Her Dog* is suggested by a sonnet of Marino; the fragments, *A Kiss; Of a Bee*, and *Hark, happy, happy Lovers, Hark!* are borrowed from Tasso, and *Upon a Glass* is suggested by a sonnet of Tasso. *The Statue of Adonis* is translated from Volpi. *To Thaumantia*, although the ultimate source is

Catullus, is adapted from the sonnet of Tasso beginning

> Viviamo, amiamci, o mia gradita Jelle
> Edra sii tu che il caro tronco abbracia.

The Rose is translated from a madrigal of Tasso, and *The Happiness of a Flea* comes from Tasso. *Constant Love* is a condensation from Watson.

The Flowers of Sion incorporates many of the flowers of foreign poetry. The first sonnet comes from one of the *Sonnets Spirituels* of Desportes; the sonnet called *No Trust in Time* is based on the twelfth of the *Sonnets Spirituels* beginning:

> La vie est une fleur espineuse et poignante,
> Belle au lever du jour, seiche en son occident,

and the sonnet entitled *Nature must lead to grace* comes also from Desportes. *The Book of the World* and the *Angels for the Nativity of Our Lord* are translated from Marino. *Amazement at the Incarnation of God* and *For the Magdalene* are translated from Desportes. *For the Magdalene* is the finest sonnet of the collection and is worthy of its model:

> De foy, d'espoir, d'amour et de douleur comblée,
> Celle que les pecheurs doivent tous imiter,
> O seigneur, vint ce jour à tes piés se jetter
> Peu craignant le mespris de toute une assemblée.

Marino inspired the sonnets entitled *For the Prodigal* and *Man's knowledge Ignorance in the Mysteries of God*, while *The World a Game* was suggested by an Italian madrigal. *An Hymn of the Fairest Fair* is an amplification of Ronsard's *Hymne de l'Eternité*, whole passages being little more than translations; and Ronsard's *Hymne de la Justice* has inspired portions of the *Shadow of the Judgment*, passages of which likewise resemble Du Bartas' *Creation en Sept Journées*.

The Pastoral Elegy on the Death of Alexander owes something to the fourth eclogue of Ronsard. *The Entertainment of King Charles* also contains reminiscences of Ronsard.

The exercises at the beginning of the *Posthumous Poems* show how Drummond could disguise his translations. The fourth of the sonnets to Galatea comes from the seventy-third of *Les Amours d'Hippolyte*:

> Si c'est aimer que porter bas la vue,
> Que parler bas, que soupirer souvent.

The Miscellanies owe much to foreign sources. The second fragment beginning thus:

It autumn was, and cheerful chanticleer
Had warned the world twice that the day drew near,

is adapted from the following passage in an elegy of Ronsard:

Nous estions en automne et já l'oiseau cresté
Qui annonce le jour deux fois avait chanté.

On a glass sent to his best beloved is also a
condensation from Passerat. Marino supplied
models for *Nero's Image*, for *A sigh*, and for *For
Dorus*. *Stolen Pleasure* is an adaptation from a
madrigal by Tasso. The subject of *Love Vaga-
bonding* was ever a favourite with Greek and
Italian poets since the time when Moschus
popularised it in his well-known idyll.

Drummond showed great skill in perceiving
the lyrical possibilities of passages of longer
poems. The madrigal beginning with the lines:

Look how in May the rose
At sulphur's azure fumes
In a short space her crimson blush doth lose

is adapted from a passage in Jodel's *Didon*.

To a swallow is adapted from some lines of
Mauritio Moro:

Garrula rondinella
Quest' è Medea crudele e ancor nol vedi;

and the version of *Venus Armed* in the Hawthornden manuscript comes under the title
"madrigali di Mauritio Moro."

The two poems *Phyllis on the death of her
Sparrow* and *Phyllis and Damon* are derived from
Passerat. The *Character of a Malignant* is

modelled as regards matter on some biting verses which Passerat proposed for the *Satire Ménippée*.

These are the plagiarisms of Drummond which cannot possibly be refuted. Others there are—plagiarisms of spirit—which indeed it is almost impossible to trace.

It is then legitimate to ask whether, in the light of modern criticism, Drummond can be regarded as a lyrical poet. The answer must emphatically be in the affirmative. Even in his unoriginality Drummond is invincibly original.

In the first place, it needs a poet to translate poetry from one language to another. The difference between the translator who is a poet and an artist, and the translator who is an artificer, may be seen from the difference in the adaptations of Drummond and Fletcher of the sonnet of Ronsard, beginning "O doux parler." Drummond's translation is poetry, Fletcher's is a mere jumble of words, rendered slightly ridiculous by the artificial affectation of enthusiasm. Lodge and Drummond were poets in their translation. The one added to the original his soft and mellifluous versification—the other his rich and varied vocabulary; for Drummond was a weaver of words.

Secondly, the selective power displayed in Drummond's versification is very strong. The imitation (for Drummond's sonnets were rarely mere mosaics, like those of Alexander) was always artistic. Jarring or hyperbolical notes in the original were almost invariably abolished by the adapter. The strength of Drummond's selective power may be seen from the nature of his translations from Passerat. What he translated is always worth translation.

Thirdly, the sonnet was less dependent on originality for excellence than any other form of poetry. The sonnet has been called "the random symbol of the soul," and the name is excellent in more ways than one. The Elizabethan sonnet has been much maligned on account of its tendency towards plagiarism and its lack of originality, but it served a definite purpose and for this purpose originality was not required.

Sonneteering was only a phase of Elizabethan poetry. The spontaneity of some of the sonnet sequences was unquestionable, but very often the "shadowy wraith" of feigned love breaks over phantasmal mistresses. Yet even if the Elizabethan sonnet sequences were frequently addressed to mythical mistresses, they are none the less a characteristic product of Renaissance literature. Like youth, they are not original, but they serve a distinct use. They are less impregnated with pessimism than Renaissance tragedy; yet they are, to a certain extent, personal, and served as a means of outlet for the vague foundationless melancholy experienced by many of the poets living in the boundlessly imaginative Elizabethan age—an outlet not afforded by the lyric poetry. Thus even if the sonneteers do not address personal mistresses, their legendary mistresses serve as the excuse for self-externalisation, as the medium for the externalising of those vague sentiments of *malaise* experienced by them. In this way the sonnet sequences of the better sonneteers can by no means be neglected by any one who desires comprehension of the spirit of the sixteenth century. In the hands of lesser writers (such as Giles Fletcher), who were dull and entirely mechanical, and who stuck to the task of describing stereotyped sensations, the sonnet sequence is tiresome. But the number of sequences that lack significance is greatly surpassed by those which do not.

Thus plagiarism, when the function of the sonnet sequence is taken into account, is not fatal to lyrical reputation. The sonnet, even if not addressed to "princesses" of real life, served as the excuse for various reflections and meditations. As the feelings expressed were more or less the common stock of the youth of the Renaissance, plagiarism was not fatal, whether the sonnets were regarded as personal love lyrics, or as mere expressions of the pain inflicted on the senses by the obsession of the "feminine" in general, or as the vehicle for the utterance of youthful philosophy. The difference between the sonnets, the feelings of all youth—and love poems which are the result of burning personal passion—is illustrated by the difference between the works of the sonneteers and the poems of Donne. As in Elizabethan literature generally there was too little silence, too little comprehension of the possibilities of silence, and no conception of the sublimity of silence, so the sonnets are somewhat theatrical in quality— "temperamental" but not distinctive, full of an impersonal pain.

The subjects of Drummond's poems are love, death and philosophy. Love and death have been fruitful sources of lyrical inspiration, but Drummond contrives to invest his working out of even these themes with a certain temperamental pallor and frigidity. The *Tears on the*

Death of Moeliades is good as a whole. The repeated lines, having a specific welding effect, reveal the metrist. Some of the best lines of the piece are the following:

> Amongst shrill sounding trumpets—flaming gleams
> Of warm encrimsoned swords, and cannons' roar

and

> From Thule to Hydaspes' pearly shore

and

> The slow Boötes turns, or sun doth rise
> With scarlet scarf to cheer the mourning skies.

In the first division of the poems we have a rich mass of poetic material. The second sonnet contains the following good lines:

> I know frail beauty like the purple flower
> To which one morn oft birth and death affords

and

> When sense and will invassal reason's power.

There are some good lines in the first song, such as:

> Far from the muddy world's captiving snares—

and

> The nymphs oft here do bring their maunds with
> flowers
> And anadems weave for their paramours.

and

> It was my hap, O woeful hap, to bide,

and

> Whose ceiling spread was with the locks of amber
> Of new bloomed sycamores,

and the description of the nymph, beginning with the lines:

> Her hair, more bright than are the morning's beams,
> Hung in a golden shower above the streams

is very fine. It lacks only rapture.

Very delightful is the madrigal:

> Like the Idalian queen,
> Her hair about her eyne
> With neck and breast's ripe apples to be seen
>   At first glance of the morn
> In Cyprian gardens gathering those fair flowers
>   Which of her blood were born,
> I saw—but fainting saw—my paramour.

The twenty-sixth sonnet contains the following finely paragraphed lines:

> Look to this dying lily, fading rose,
> Dark hyacinth, of late whose blushing beams
> Made all the neighbouring herbs and grass rejoice.

The seventh madrigal is very fine as regards metre:

>   Unhappy light
> Do not approach to bring the woful day
>   When I must bid for ay
>   Farewell to her and live in endless plight.

The second division of the Poems is equally

rich in good lyrical passages. The second sonnet
contains the lines:

> Those locks of gold, that purple fair of Tyre,
> Are wrap't—ay me—up in eternal night.

Sonnet four is good:

> O woful life. Life? No but living death,
> Frail boat of crystal in a rocky sea!

The first madrigal is particularly beautiful:

> This life, which seems so fair,
> Is like a bubble blown up in the air
> By sporting children's breath
> Who chase it everywhere.

The first song contains the line:

> Benighted set into a sea of tears

and the lyrical outburst:

> O Pan, Pan, winter is fallen in our May,
> Turned is in night our day.

Drummond never wrote anything better than
the almost impassioned paragraph which follows:

> That zephyr every year
> So soon was heard to sigh in forests here
> It was for her: that wrapt in gown of green
> Meads were so early seen,
> That in the saddest months oft rang the merles
> It was for her: for her trees dropt forth pearls.
> That proud and stately courts
> Did envy those our shades and calm resorts
> It was for her: and she is gone, O woe!
> Woods cut again do grow,
> Bud doth the rose and daisy, winter done,
> But we once dead, no more do see the sun.

The excellence of the style of sonnet ten is marked. The best two lines are:

What doth it serve to hear the sylvan songs,
The wanton merle, the nightingale's sad strain?

Sonnet twelve contains the two fine lines which follow:

Till ugly death, depriving us of light,
In his grim misty arms thee did enfold.

Many of the madrigals and epigrams are exceedingly dainty. The *Flowers of Sion* contain many fine passages. The *Permanency of Life* contains the lines:

Life a right shadow is
For if it long appear
Then is it spent, and life's long night draws near.

No Trust in Time begins charmingly—

Look how the flower which lingeringly doth fade.

The finest of the sonnets is the one entitled *For the Magdalene*, which ends with the lines:

Thus sigh'd to Jesus the Bethanian fair
His tear-wet feet still drying with her hair.

In the *Hymn of the Passion*, the welding effect of the repeated "if" is remarkable.

The following passage:

The sun from sinful eyes hath veil'd his light,
And faintly journeys up heaven's sapphire path;
And cutting from her brows her tresses bright
The moon doth keep her Lord's sad obsequies
Impearling with her tears this robe of night,

vaguely recalls the manner of Shelley.

The opening of the *Hymn of the Ascension*

Bright portals of the sky
Embossed with sparkling stars,
Doors of eternity
With diamantine bars

is very good.

The *Hymn of True Happiness* contains the
fine lines:

Not happy is that life
Which ye as happy hold,
No, but a sea of fears, a field of strife.

The *Pastoral Elegy* contains some good lines:

Whilst violets with purple paint the spring

and

And to their sorrows hither bring your maunds
Charged with sweetest flower, and with pure hands,
Fair nymph, the blushing hyacinth and rose,
Spread on the place his relics doth enclose.

Of the poems in the Miscellanies, *Phyllis on
the Death of her Sparrow* and *Phyllis and Damon*
are the most charming. The best of the

epitaphs is that one on a drunkard, taken from Guarini.

Coming to a general consideration of Drummond's poetry, we are at once struck by its artificial nature. Drummond was hardly a Scotsman. He was not in sympathy with his country in its time of *Sturm und Drang*. He turned away from the traditions of Scottish poetry. He turned his back even on what was good in the poetry of his predecessors. At a time when Spenser had forged out of the old and the new an incomparable poetic vocabulary, he disowned the old, and owing to his apostacy the " river of oblivion " swept its waters over Scottish poetry for more than a century and a half.

Drummond was an anomaly. Middle Scots poetry never was of the Renaissance; and although Drummond, like his friend Alexander, drew inspiration from the Italianate school of poetry, his inspiration is so thin that he cannot be called in reality a child of the Renaissance.

The reasons of the "thinness" of Drummond's muse appear when his poetry is compared with the poetry of the Pléiades and with Elizabethan poetry. Drummond was a classicist; so were the poets of the Pléiade. But Drummond was a classicist because his message was not powerful enough to endanger the perfection of his form, while the Pléiadists were inspired by the sense of the poignant beauty of earthly things, and of their evanescence, by the necessity of gripping something from the varied imagery of life and of embodying in their verse something of the soul of things sensuous and material. The poets of the Pléiade and Drummond share alike the passion for harmony and for order. But the poets of the Pléiade are classicists not because their message was too thin to imperil clearness of expression, but because they preferred clarity of outline to vague mysticism—clearly defined order to the suggestiveness of symbolism, perfection of workmanship to the vague opening out of new vistas. They preferred to dwell on the doctrine of the omnipotency of the present, to which they could give clear expression—which they could enunciate with precision—rather than to dwell on the vague disquiet which it is difficult to express in the more precise forms of verse.

And Drummond differs from the Elizabethans, though for a different reason. The Elizabethan lyrists to a certain extent imitated the French. In their sonnet cycles, they imitated French models fairly closely. But Elizabethan lyric does not in spirit imitate French lyric. Much

Elizabethan lyric, like that of Drummond, is metrical experiment; much again is Euphuistic trifling, mere weaving of words. Although there are many sparkling little lyrics, it is not until we come to Campion, Donne and Ben Jonson—to men who found a prepared instrument—that we get lyric comparable to the Pléiade lyric—the very "wind and fire" of versification conjoined to poetical thought.

But Drummond in imitating Elizabethan lyric imitated what was merely the part of an organism. The result in his case was artificial— although Elizabethan lyric in itself was not artificial, holding as it did a related place in the scheme of Elizabethan literature. The romanticism of the Elizabethans and their questionings of the future, their sense of the "love that is stronger than death" or conventional morality, their probings of the universe—go into the drama. Their sense of comedy, that strong condiment, their comic humour—went into the novels. Their rather inconsequent lightness and un- reasoned melancholy went into their lyrics. When Drummond began to write, therefore, he played belatedly only on one string. His themes were not many. Death and love are the subjects of most of his lyrics, but he does not write with the poignancy of the Pléiade poets—and there is a gulf fixed between the pale love he depicts and the mighty, burning, all-powerful, degrading love of Shakespeare's sonnets—the love that is a flame, the love that makes of morality and of the world only a species of unimpressive background. Drummond's love is merely the love of the Renaissance sonneteers. One might have expected him, writing merely lyric as he did, and having no other outlet, as had the Elizabethans, for the "lyric emotions of the soul," to have woven more into his poetry than he did. But he was Scotch, not English—and he chose to be English, and to write English poetry without tradition on his side, and, in consequence, he is merely a tuneful warbler, artist and artificer. His poems are only "a foison of fruitless" if tuneful flowers.

Scott, Montgomerie, and Drummond are excellent, all three, on the formal side, but it is to be doubted if they were of the breed of artists "who must break their heart or sing." Except in the case of Montgomerie, it is to be doubted if their poetry was inspired by genuine lyrical emotion, and even the "delicate love sheaf" of Montgomerie's poems was inspired by emotion rather than by passion. They are not the poets of fire and flame, of secret mysterious pleasure, of the " white hot hour." Their art is not the art at which the soul exults, but the art which the mind perhaps rather distantly acknowledges.

Drummond was more cosmopolitan than Scott or Montgomerie. Yet the infinite exhilaration of the Renaissance has passed him by as it failed to reach his predecessors. He fails to share alike in the happiness of the Renaissance and in its outworn Epicureanism.

By Drummond's time the old comic story with its huge jokes had gone astray, and the thin, flippant, indecent epigram satisfied the cravings of the humorous spirit.

In the sonnets of Drummond passion is outlawed. Woman is seen through the haze of Petrarchian emotion. There is nothing of the rapture of the poetry of the French Renaissance— nothing of the desire that is as sharp as a pang.

In Drummond the infinitely caressing touch of the lyric poetry of the Pléiades is lacking. Montgomerie has in a greater degree than either Scott or Drummond this curious caressing note.

The school of Middle Scots lyrists that drew their inspiration from Elizabethan sources is decadent in its inception. The glow that animates Drummond's poetry is the flare of decadence. Drummond chose to follow an almost played-out tradition. He began to follow the sonneteering vogue at a time when a species of sclerosis, the forerunner of disuse, was overtaking the sonnet with its immutable conventions.

Frugality of language was unknown to Drummond. His thinness is the thinness of poverty—not the severity, the impressive austerity, that comes from self-restraint. Occasionally the note of the second best is sounded. A kind of literary self-consciousness appears, a self-consciousness unknown in the work of the artist forcing words to yield themselves to a genuine inspiration.

The gleam of the Elizabethan school of Scotch sonneteers was transitory, as its inspiration was not indigenous and its beauty in great measure the beauty of workmanship. Except in Montgomerie the cheer if exquisite was somewhat cold. Witchery of language is not everything in poetry; and the mechanical production of sonnets, telling over the same sentiments and emotions like the telling over of the same rosary, came to be ridiculed. The beauty of the school became a little frayed—a little outworn. In

Scotland after Drummond a "mortal languour" fell upon the national poetry. For a century and a half there was no poet of consequence.

English poetry did not fare so badly. The virility of Donne, drunken with passion, making his lyric the medium of expressing burning human and personal passion, broke the Petrarchian tradition. The love Donne portrays is not "the ideal love of Dante, nor the refined sentiment of Petrarch: nor the chivalrous love of Sidney." It is a feeling of intoxication and of half physical, half metaphysical excitement, not to be compared with the impersonal emotion of the sonneteers. The advent of Donne in England has been compared to the advent of Michael Angelo in early Florentine art. Genuine passion and genuine inspiration burnt away from the soul of lyric its draperies of unnecessary ornament and stereotyped phrasing. For the faint pleasure of Euphuistic trifling, for the heavy beauty of chryselephantine treatment (common rather in Scotch than in English poetry), we have once more lyrics fiery, direct, clear-cut, clamant; lyrics whose beauty is independent of the charm lent by "the fopperies of diction," lyrics which voice the mysterious and intangible emotions of the soul. Truly with Drummond the sonneteering era with all it represented passed away, as the characteristic glories of the school of Middle Scots poets, whose inspiration was genuinely mediaeval, made their final appearance in the work of Alexander Montgomerie—the Last of the Makars.

Printed in the United States
By Bookmasters